RABBIT HOLES
A Collection of Golden Shovel Poems

Robert E. Ray

Copyright © 2025 by Robert E. Ray

All rights reserved. No part of this book may be used or reproduced by any means, graphic, electronic, or mechanical, including photocopying, recording, taping or by any information storage retrieval system without the written permission of the publisher, except the brief quotations embodied in critical articles and reviews.

for *you*

rabbit hole *noun*

a complexly bizarre or difficult state or situation conceived of as a hole into which one falls or descends

especially: one in which the pursuit of something (such as an answer or solution) leads to other questions, problems, or pursuits

Merriam-Webster. (n.d.). Rabbit hole. In Merriam-Webster.com dictionary. Retrieved September 28, 2025, from https://www.merriam-webster.com/dictionary/rabbit%20hole

golden shovel *poem*

a form of contemporary poetry, devised by Terrance Hayes, where each line of a new poem ends with a word from a line taken from an existing poem or song. The poet keeps the words in their original order, creating a *shovel* of words down the right margin of the page, and gives credit to the original writer. This poetic exercise serves as a way to engage with and pay tribute to another poet or songwriter's work while challenging the poet's creativity.

Poetry Foundation. Golden shovel. In Glossary of Poetic Terms. Retrieved October 12, 2025, from
https://www.poetryfoundation.org/education/glossary/golden-shovel

I shall create! If not a note, a hole.

—Gwendolyn Brooks

Hanging Out in a No-Name Pub

after William Butler Yeats' The Mermaid

My destination was a gift shop, next door to a
historic pub, a green-eyed fisherman & mermaid
wood carving over a pitted oak transom. I found
him on a creaky stool, in a musty wool suit, a
monogram on his left cuff, cherry swimming
mid-crystal in his whiskey. On the far left, a lad
cozied up to his doe-eyed honey. *WBY* picked
up his tumbler and slurped. I was with him
when he choked on that engorged cherry and for
hours of flights of malts and single pots. Her
half love had held him, that woman, not his own
who'd rejected him for decades. I pressed
him. Why not give up, not free himself and her
of the heart's burden? He said his whole body
of work came from his deep desire for her, to
persuade her that his love was true, that his
poetry was not halfhearted, that his body
and words were hers. We got drunk and laughed
about the lad's man-bun, her creeping butterfly, and
the free-verse fad. WBY reached over me, plunging
one hand into the big pickled egg jar, down
to the bottom and pulled out the fattest. I forgot
why I'd gone out, why I'd walked a mile in
the rain—a Hallmark card for her. But how cruel
it'd be to leave WBY alone in that pub. Happiness
bloomed on his cheeks like wet pink roses that
moment, when I recited that ottava rima—even
though I mispronounced *Byzantium*. Those lovers
fled in a downpour, us sure the lad would drown.

Red

after Ted Hughes

My study is wall to wall red
like the *salvia*, the blood sage, was
when the beekeeper derived your
name. I read you liked the colour.

I see lines and needles only
pressure and light gauges on the
dashboard. My cherry bookshelves
hold your spine. *Ariel* has escaped
down the black dead-end road, into
the woods, the moon's waning whiteness.

I don't get *substanceless blue*.
I assume whatever it was
or was not (like smoke) was better
air. I don't write poetry for
the art of it or because of you

or her. Outdoors, the bees and blue
bellflowers buzz and dance. I was
seed when you found your primrose wings.

The Waste Land

after T.S. Eliot

We wake late, swallow green pills, lattes, blue pills. There are new texts and old games to play. The a.m. slog is time to drone on, and eat and drink (more), and smoke the next cigarette. The fridge and bank account are empty. They buried Cousin Sam in his dress blues by the chapel. A camouflaged brown man squats curbside; he holds his only palm up; he catches cold raindrops, sticky pennies, the lint from my left pocket. Tinfoil rustles in the wind's last huff. On the landfill there's a school and our home.

As usual, the azaleas bloomed first of March. April rain washes away the pink and the dog shit. It is what greens the grass, yellows the dandelions, brings the swollen worms and kitten skulls to the surface—cruellest to the new widow expecting tulips spring's first full month.

All My Pretty Ones

after Anne Sexton

These days I'm trending towards minimalism. I
covet matches and fire. You crave the touch
and flash of conveniences. We disagree on their
value. We agreed to keep the old cardboard
shoeboxes of photos. We recognize the faces
the young bodies in fractions. Scattered, they
lie on hardwood in quarter light. They must
find a new home. We disagree where they'll go.

Then, I rarely smiled. You rarely frowned. These
truths haven't changed. Our moods are
a full set of teeth. On the polished floor the
loose make a collage. Polaroid snapshots
pass through our fingers like money of
the 90s. The beginning was not marriage
but a moon spot in the woods where we stopped
time. Now, late-day the new baby lies in
the sun, milk-breath coos in the empty places.

At Darien Bridge

after James L. Dickey

It was an April morning of birds. I
flew by dozens on four tires. Trash was
strewn in the ditches. Loose chickens pecked in
mowed-down weeds and day-lilies. Crows lined this
stretch of high wires. Low tide, out in the bog
blue herons and white egrets came & went as
homeless vets in the city park, a
crooked fence row of starlings drew a child
near the four-lane highway. I don't know when
or where these birds nest, wake or take off (they
don't fly a predictable route). They were
white and black and pink in blue, some, not all
arranged like war planes. I was working
my way through traffic, orange cones, all
lined up like rubber-neck tourists. The day
began and ended on the same bridge to
bog birds, and buzzards 'round a hog—same drive
backwards. In the ditches, chickens pecked the
trash, two pelicans stooped on bald pilings
of a gone pier, watching for fish way down.

After Apple-Picking

after Robert Frost

It's too hot for apples. The last frost, late for
south Georgia, killed the first blueberry crop I
had long looked forward to picking. Now we have
purpleless limbs, save a few handfuls. We had
hopes of rows of drums, freezers full (never too
few to share with neighbors). Still, there is much
to be thankful for. The green fields are full of
sun and good soil. Sundays, we dine on apple
pie, drink cider, and pray for mid-year picking
a second crop of rabbit eyes, berries I
turn into sweet wines. The neighbors think I am
a sinner. I'm a believer, overtired
from haters. I'm a man of the black dirt, of
a higher being. She and I pray for the
next reap. We know the taste & fullness of great
fruit, endless flesh & seed from a purple harvest.

Edge of the fields, I
watch sun rise, rain fall—myself
blood & body desired.

Overflowing

after Du Fu

Anchor down, rope taut, I rigged the hook. Behind
us, the ripples smoothed, the full moon turned the
brown water silver. A cool gust spun the wood boat
counterclockwise; reoriented, I
aimed short of the white-haired cattails. We could hear
the turtles sliding off mud-banked logs, the
whippoorwill overhead, the croak and splash
of a frog in the lilies—purple sky full of
crows cawing over the cotton field, a jumping
cricket's chirp end in the mouth of a moonward fish.

The View from the Road

after Robert Pinsky

I wake in the gray. It's time to head home. From
here it's four days of stop and go to the
indent in the mountain, where the junk pink car
rests nose-down in the creek. The landscapes
change each mile up, right, then left, momently
a river view, then rockface; I recede
into the granite and evergreens, the
dank shadows of Appalachia. Scrub trees
hanging off the dynamited rock are
like wide-eyed base jumpers & suicidals, an
assured freefall into the arcade
three thousand feet down, silver river of
feldspar, quartz and trout, rainbows in motion.
It's too many months before the wild sweet
blackberries stain fingers, reasonable
to eat directly from the green thickets, and
where the trespassers creep in low and fast
to steal the ginseng. It's a return that
is long overdue. The family orchard is
neglected ground now, but I still recall how
we'd sneak in late and drink fruit jars of shine, you
would curl in those white petals, and how I'd drive
us out first hint of dawn, sun low, eastbound for home.

An Aspect of Love, Alive in the Ice and Fire

after Gwendolyn Brooks

It's been ages since we were *We*
though you stay because I make you laugh
every day, you say. It's no joke: We
know it's important to laugh and touch
(not only when we're drunk). *To each
his/her/their own! (*This is the other
me: half woke/half ass.) Any night's a
good night to get physical
when we're buzzing—the bedside light
off. *You look better in the dark* is
truth spoken—what we both say in
our half bemoaning way. It's true: the
old flames rage & cool in the same room.

What Work Is

after Philip Levine

Steel toed, blue jeaned, shirtless, half bronze, we scaled the steep pitched black roofs. Now I stand bent, foot of a wood ladder, deep pains in most joints. The tawny sun splotches are the signs of aging; a half bald oak in spring rain wind beaten and baked by the gold rays in heights of past summers. The hammer & nail is a weapon. I kill every job! Blue chalk and long string help me keep the heads in a straight line.

Feast

after Edna St. Vincent Millay

We met at that Chicago brownstone. I
saw her in the paneled parlor. She drank
ate and moved like an African lioness. At
midnight her boy date called a cab. Every
man watched her wink and slink out. A vine

across the cobblestone caught her heel, the
cab sped off. I rushed in. I didn't last
long that first night. Still, she swore I was
her true love. (She'd teach me.) I wasn't like
the others. In my coupe, we cruised down the
shore at sunset. Loons fished. I was her first

southern lover, she swore. She didn't say I
would be her last. Now, at high tide, I will
drive along the Savannah coast, and I'll lie
under the old magnolias. She'll be down
on her back in white silk. I'll stay lean
on dreams and whiskey; I'll get on without her. I once whispered she'd be my
one and only. But her verses cause a thirst
I can't quench with sweet memories and
broken moonlight. She'll always be my
desired feast—but not my last hunger.

The Secret Garden

after Rita Dove

Through the unblinded window panes, I watch her weed on her bare knees. The lawn was invaded by prickly thistle & yellow nutsedge; ill cedars still line the property. They were lying when they sold us this American foursquare on an Easter-Sunday handshake. I won't waste my time killing an unwanted thing. The rose bed sleeps black, weedy, and wilted red. Petals of last autumn cradle the fallen acorns. That old spade knifes new green—this pen, these papers.

Digging

after Seamus Heaney

Billy and I off loaded the locust posts by
the road. We labored after Sunday church. God
understood, dad said. He handed over the
post-hole diggers—after measuring twice. Old
blue china came up with red clay and sludge. A man
parked along the yellow curb; that pastor could
go on for hours. I dug. One mudded wood handle
of the two splintered on a thick black root, a
passable reason to rest. Dad picked up the spade.

Lines for Winter

after Mark Strand

for Emily

Shame it snowed the week of your birthday. Tell
yourself it's white rain for snowdrops, tell yourself
those emerald blades will rise and triumph in
that gray haze of winter's last gasp, that
dandelions make very good victory wine, the final
snow melt is the past, all the dead-reek flowing
down the Wabash, into the bigger river. Clouds of
blackbirds are good omens—and the cold
air warming is the lonely cardinal's song through
the yellowing hedgerow, uphill—beyond your
pickets, where wild blackberries on bowed limbs
of pricks make sweet summer wine, and that
fallen pink from the dogwoods cover the mud you
cross—like plodding through a poem you don't love
but you go on, head up. Grace and grit are what
make you the perennial heartbeat of spring. You
girl, are the red on a rain flower. April's who you are.

Morning Song

after Sylvia Plath

in honor of Frieda Hughes, painter and poet

A raised bedside window and warm milk: Love
in its final act, the gas-lit stage set
for your father's solo performance, you
and Nick ticketed back to Court Green, going
where your mother painted little hearts like
a school girl on the used furniture, a
hundred faded red splotches from a fat
sore thumb and bandaged finger, single gold
band same hand as that winding-down watch.

Blue Motel Room

after Joni Mitchell

You're gone this gray April Monday. It's lonely here in this one red-light town. After one sad song, I'm in my pickup, one Patsy Cline playlist from Savannah miles of pine flanked blacktop and yellow dashes; it's too far and too close. I've made a bad habit of pouring time into nothing—good whiskey into coke. The rain dimples the beach, gulls squawk for cheese crackers. I've got no business driving, no plastic to uber home. I've got no reservations, no close-by friends. Truck keys lost, a fluorescent light down the street flickers *VAC NCY*—blue neon flashes inside that diner. It's the same 90s motel same plastic violets—two young lovers in our first room.

The Crunch

after Charles Bukowski

I like only about a dozen people.
No lawyers. No bankers. No politicians. They are
the problem. Not god. Not the laws. Not
money. Not elections. The homeless must be good
people. They haven't broken in to
take mine. They share thrown-out boxes with each
other. We mostly screw over each other.

I like beer and donuts and cracker jacks. People
blow money and drink and eat too many. They are
pigs. Pigs are not the problem. And not
beer, not donuts, not cracker jacks. Good
beer, donuts, and salty & sweet nuts are easy to
find. In boxes they get along with each
other. We mostly screw over each other.

I like pain killers but flush them. People
take too many, like other drugs. They are
potheads and losers and family. They are not
my friends. They are not the problem. Good
people do bad things, like song birds do to
worms—and the worms to the fish. Each
end up on our hooks. We make them screw each other.

The Revisionist Dream

after Maxine Kumin

I have not forgotten nor forgiven you. We
talked—you promised the week before. We ate
hot wings with blue cheese and drank beer with our
brothers & sisters. Those fishy po-boy sandwiches
that redhead bartender served us were cold. The
azaleas had bloomed in south Georgia; the dream
ended with one finger. That spring storm blew
ice on the glass like a shotgun blast. I woke up
freezing three states away, sipped hotel coffee at
the frosted window—no birdsong at dawn.

Away

after James Whitcomb Riley

What god grew this beauty with shapely legs? She
wears a split cherry top. Her bottom half is
heart pine aged to gold. I like to show off not
her drawers but the pretty keyholes. But she's dead
legged, whiskey ringed and smoky. Silently, she
lies under my hand. I fill the last sheet; it is
a tattoo on her skin. I drop the pen. She's not just
tired but worn bare. By candle, the words run away.

75mg

after June Johnson

a young woman in blue scrubs slid me in
the cool white tube, smooth jazz in my ears, my
eyes covered, tiles and walls pigeon grey
like the ceiling and cracked walls in the house.
they gave me advil and a pillow. i
wanted an opioid. i felt cold air blow
through the grey vents. i smelled cigarette smoke
through the glass. i put on my watch and rings
(time, college, and marriage mean something). at
the window a pale old man grimaced, the
rivers & roads on a face in the mirror.
i went to the truck, then to
the bar. i drank two. i know
what street cops ask about that.
the old bartender said i
spent too much time in there. am
i a drunk? again, i'm at
a breaking point. but at least
i have good health care. real
pain is in needing and
nothing. i wanted to swallow
a purple oxy and the
third whiskey. the bleach-blonde white
girl at the grill worked for the pill
dealer down the road. knowing
they'd never sell to me, hope
slipped like the six o'clock sun is
expected in spring. it's not
night that scares me but a
dark house, a dead finch on the side-
porch—the whiskey cause and effect.

a map to the next world

after Joy Harjo

only the old and broken know what's crucial
for the young and unscarred go whole head-first to
the center of everything. there's no finding
peace in the crowd. you are the fledgling on the
wing. in the bush you lose your way
in the dark and prickly things. the path is
faith. listen!—the wind whispers this:
sleep with the sun, rise with the moon; there
in the long shadows, trailing and leading, is
your past and future—no
present. unfold in light. find your beginning
on the empty fringe. go there or
against the tide. go where there's no end

The Killing

after Charles Wright

We necked alongside that farmer's pond and
walked the cattailed dam. Below the nightshade
we kissed again and fell into the foxtail. "They
look sweet," she said, reaching out. I didn't say
the fruit was toxic. We eyed fireflies. Truth is
silent in those moments. I was sure
we'd kiss again. Gold flickered in her hair. Two
a.m., we woke, the belladonna berries
shined like cherries in the full moonlight. "You can
drop me at the corner—or my dad will kill
you," she said. With her shawl she covered a
purple stain on her skirt. I wasn't quite a man.

Windows

after Charles Baudelaire

Next door the little children spill out
after the rain, their pink fists full of
sweets and Easter trinkets from her
the stranger who always turns her face
away from us; no hellos from her
no waves or nods. The smallest girl's dress
balloons in wind—a yellow sail and
pony-tail maiden in a green sea; her
spirit fits the day. Our gestures
go unnoticed. One boy bikes out
into the puddled street, one hand full of
white rabbit ears. He's practically
naturalizing it. It's nothing
out of the ordinary for boys at
play and war. Off to the park they all
five go for the Easter egg hunt. I
watch through the clearing panes. They have
stories I don't get. Truth: I have made
poetry from lies. When the sun comes up
this house is half empty. Standing at this
sunned window I catch glimmers, the woman's
gold cross, the star behind glass—her story.

Apples in Early October

after Dave Smith

There's no bird song this Sunday morning; it
is a gunshot that wakes me. It comes
like a door slamming down the hall; it's the
neighbor woman, with a rifle, dawn's faint
light on her face, apple-red, nothing sweet
anger instead. There's an autumn bloodscent
in the wind, the familiar whiff of
gunpowder, another squirrel, the rot
of flesh under the porch floorboards; it comes
up through the dark cracks between the pine, it
is what the dogs killed the day before. It is
the same reek, the orchard in October
where fallen pecans split open & rot, and
above the nuts, the buzzards know something
has died for them. The orchard keeper has
fled. The bird on the wire knows what's happened.

Apples in the bowl
softening brown, catch the light.
The redbird's quiet.
In the orchard, a squirrel
gnaws through fire ants and green skin.

All The World's A Stage

after William Shakespeare

Commuters gone, I walk along Peachtree, all the closer parking spaces taken, the planes dropping in, lifting off from the world's busiest airport. Renaissance Park is a hopeful name; a few blocks from the stage of The Shakespeare Tavern Playhouse—and where real life is a tragedy. All sorts show up and audition; some sleep on the streets. In a cool rain six camouflaged men congregate under a brown awning and share a pack of cigarettes, two wrinkled women in black bags linger by the alley (it's merely a measure to stay dry). The night's players use the coded side door, camera light on; they go heads bowed, talking with thumbs. I have no skills or will to match them. It's their tattoos I admire most. A pretty girl exits. I see her low-waistline pink butterfly and Old English script in green. Two people in their tuxes kiss in a black Mercedes. Two entrances have the same sign: **No Firearms**; a gun and the state law in bold red. I carry one everywhere. I hand my two tickets to a man pushing a yellow plastic cart. I say, "Go in and enjoy the show." For five bucks I buy his peach wine. I sit in the *Fire Zone* at show time. Curbside, I smell piss and shit. The night plays on. My wine man's thrown out. (I pity many and myself.) The doors open, the crowd parts.

Wondering Why

after The Red Clay Strays

Three hours before daybreak I'm awake. She's
now mumbling unintelligibly, not
anything about me, us, or this, just
frivolous chatter, utterances along
the lines of the padded-room crazies, for
stories later over lattes, posts, the
early birdsong, morning buzz, vibes I'll ride
grateful for our time, her laugh, and when she's
gone, lost in texts, what I miss the most, my
irreverent humor for her biggest
brightest smile—truth being, I was a fan
years before she knew my name, before she
mouthed that four-letter word, language that keeps
steam on these two-pane windows, my eyes on
indigo, my smudged page, blue pen, loving
more what she gifts me
new breaths into a seized chest, each and
every stroke an inexplicable blessing I
revisit, as ancient cave art I keep
uncovering, familiar blood smears on
azure dawns, as I keep wondering
looking back, past her—undeniably my why.

Turn the Page

after Bob Seger

The sun sunk behind the motel. I arrived later
than planned. The clerk and her man were in
the gravel lot, yellow hood propped up on the
dropped-down Cadillac. She worked evening
shift. He hung out. They checked me out as
I backed in my truck and plodded in. "Do you
have a reservation?" she asked. (I don't lie
usually.) And I didn't tell her I'd been awake
four days. Inside, I caught my reflection in
the glassed-over watercolor. I wanted a bed
and hot water for a shower, a bug-free room with
views of the creek and greening mountains, the
blue fog like a halo. Down the dogwalk: echoes
from a domestic spat or rough sex. From
behind plexiglass, she asked my name—the
windows rattled from her man's amplifiers
his rap music cranked up—a burner ringing
in her back pocket. The boyfriend slunk in
reeking of body odor and weed. "What's your
name?" I handed her a fifty, my turned head
a thousand miles down the highway. "And you
need an ID," she said. I wanted to smoke
something illegal. I glanced at her man in the
foyer. Surely, he had a few dime bags, a day's
wages from the roofers and hookers. The last
room was by the ice machine, wet cigarette
butts piled by the red door. I was remembering
the first I-75 motel room with her, what
we ate, the cheap beer we drank, the *Bob* she
loved in bed. *Checkout:* XXX, the placard said.

Majesty

after Warpaint

Vicariously, I live through *its*. So
when those pad-and claw prints show up you
become the *it* I zero on. I let
myself become dumb prey. Do you hear me
stumble up and down these trails, see me slip
and fall, smell me, before you steal away?
Truth: I was not born for this hardness. You
came wild-eyed, leather-soled, hungry, fur just
tawny enough to seem stone, where you've watched
lesser meat-eaters kneel and pray like me.
Noon, I glimpse it, grooming, then rise and walk
the gorge. *It* zeroes in. None get away.

white horse

after Chris Stapleton

nobody told me i would die like this
rivers and whiskey are two things i love
and horses—but this tributary is
too turbulent right here and it's getting
higher and wilder, breakers of the kind
unconquered in the foggy gorges of
the chattooga, where it's more dangerous
to climb up and out. the pearly mist feels
its way over to me, a strange sting like
her hello and goodbye in one kiss. it's
certainly autumn, moonrise sooner; a
white horse crowns the ridge, bituminous sky loaded
with pink elephants—the river hemingway's gun.

Love You Anyway

after Luke Combs

We've come to this mountain to rest. Even
ground isn't found here. You know you must dig, if
you want softer earth to lay your head. I
stir orange coals and watch you sleep. You knew
I'd do this, protect and serve you, the
role of a *good man*, so I was taught day
and night, year after year. *Tradition*—we
accept because it's worked out. If we'd met
in an earlier time, we be here; you'd
wrap yourself in handwoven wool and be
dreaming just as deeply. I'd *man* the
fire with a hand-forged Bowie, reason
stretched beneath the white smoke and glow of this
fire. About the size of a fist, the heart
I've heard—so I don't get how the thing *breaks*.
I read by flame, Teasdale's *Wind and Rain*, "Oh
but the wind can be a soft friend." I'd
wake you before the storm comes but I love
how wildly your hair dances in wind, how you
turn into the rain and sleep anyway.

Over the Hills and Far Away

after Led Zeppelin

Don't say it's too late, too many
miles. We can sail there in our dreams
Look behind you, how far you've come
I believe all you've said is true
Would you believe it? I've seen and
climbed that Spanish tower some
Roman architect drew. I have
looked out, seen the water silver
hills purple as royal linings
of a Herculean robe. I
once danced in the streets to the live
music of locals, and sang for
a beaut from Portugal when my
heart outdrank my head. I still dream
about my first Queimada and
birthday in La Coruña, a
red-eye flight home, a pocketful
of pesetas, The Seven Hills of
San Francisco and that gate of gold.

*I saw you riding shotgun
shooting into the sun*

She's My Kind of Rain

after Tim McGraw

Our first love's a season, summer
crickets and sticky nights, hot days
of pink, cherry skin, our winter
memories closeted, last snow
a swollen river we swim. She's
still there, in chin-deep whitewater, all
in, nothing on, whispering things
memories, fantasies, scents to
bottle, one fragrance to behold
honeysuckle on one pillow. She's
one happy, two sad songs on my
rock and roll and jazz playlists, kind
of poetry I read when the rain
makes music on the tin roof, like
Picasso's Blue Period, love
lingering after the last words from
her tongue, smudged rouge morning lips, a
river of verse to a drunken
man, head over heels, eyes in the sky.

Take Me Away

after Morgan Wade

Trust is the boarded window, the door I've
bolted and chained, the two-story I've been
rebuilding myself within. I'm looking
for a mirror I didn't shatter, for
my Bowie knife, scout compass, some
cedar-crowned mountain, one-room cabin, peace
I can't find in a bar or bottle of
Kentucky's finest bourbon, where my mind
can roam like a feral Appaloosa, and
sleep comes on a copper-needle mat, a bed with
a view of Venus and the North Star, you
stirring the stone-circled fire. You're here
there, wherever I lie and rise. I
know nothing really. I think
love: apricity, ubiquity, rarity, Eros, nonpareil; it's
a new mountain greening, spring, our time.

Epilogue

after Robert Lowell

This very form speaks cemeteries. We
are loath to lay such plot and rhyme. These are
the words of a dead poet. And how poor
this choice. His voice triggers a skunk passing
faintness from ether; the medical facts
of his mental state ransacked. He warned
us about the *confessional* thing, by
berating Sylvia Plath, saying that
she was "a miniature mad talent." And to
his point, he schooled her, and later he'd give
her and Sexton fragments of his mind, each
hour one madder, each one now a figure
of speech, similes and metaphors in
undeniable pleas for help, and the
worst new verse. Each conjures a photograph
old stereotypes, hysteria, *his
mad wife* first, *poet* last. Me? I'm living
gravely, chiseling my own face and name.

Aristotle

after Billy Collins

This is not about Aristotle (or you).

It's people outside the theater. This
is the pond before I arrive; it is
the calm water, dragonflies buzzing, the
fish in the cattails, a frog's beginning.

It's Plath's *peanut-crunching crowd.* Sobbing. This
is six of twelve beers, a half pint; it is
a half-worm gold hook, a hard tug on the
line, the ripples rolling out from the middle.

It's the gray coroner showing up, and
an empty red cooler, melted ice. This
is a hole, no mirror image; it is
fried fish and hushpuppies, crows cawing, the
oaks and sky black, cigar smoke, April's end.
This is not (truly) a *golden shovel*
but a loud thwack, a broken wood handle
—a rusted spoon in the black dirt after...

> And the end of all our exploring
> Will be to arrive where we started
> And know the place for the first time.
> — T. S. Eliot, *Four Quartets*

The End

www.ingramcontent.com/pod-product-compliance
Lightning Source LLC
LaVergne TN
LVHW041550070426
835507LV00011B/1016